Fun Mother's Day Crafts

Kid Fun Holiday Crafts!

Arlene and Herbert Erlbach

Enslow Elementary
an imprint of
Enslow Publishers, Inc.
40 Industrial Road
Box 398
Berkeley Heights, NJ 07922
USA
http://www.enslow.com

Enslow Elementary, an imprint of Enslow Publishers, Inc.
Enslow Elementary® is a registered trademark of Enslow Publishers, Inc.

Originally published as *Mother's Day Crafts* in 2005.

Library of Congress Cataloging-in-Publication Data

Erlbach, Arlene, author.
  [Mother's day crafts]
  Fun Mother's Day crafts / Arlene and Herbert Erlbach.
      pages cm. — (Kid fun holiday crafts!)
  "Originally published as Mother's Day Crafts in 2005."
  Summary: "Explains the origins of Mother's Day and how to make ten holiday-related crafts."— Provided by publisher.
  Audience: K to grade 3.
  Includes bibliographical references and index.
  ISBN 978-0-7660-6245-0
  1. Mother's Day—Juvenile literature. 2. Holiday decorations—Juvenile literature. 3. Handicraft—Juvenile literature. I.
      Erlbach, Herb, author. II. Title.
  TT900.H6E74 2015
  745.594'1628—dc23
                              2014023469

Future editions:
Paperback ISBN: 978-0-7660-6246-7
Single-User PDF ISBN: 978-0-7660-6248-1

EPUB ISBN: 978-0-7660-6247-4
Multi-User PDF ISBN: 978-0-7660-6249-8

Printed in the United States of America
102014 Bang Printing, Brainerd, Minn.
10 9 8 7 6 5 4 3 2 1

To Our Readers: We have done our best to make sure all Internet addresses in this book were active and appropriate when we went to press. However, the author and the publisher have no control over and assume no liability for the material available on those Internet sites or on other Web sites they may link to. Any comments or suggestions can be sent by e-mail to comments@enslow.com or to the address on the back cover.

♻ Enslow Publishers, Inc., is committed to printing our books on recycled paper. The paper in every book contains 10% to 30% post-consumer waste (PCW). The cover board on the outside of each book contains 100% PCW. Our goal is to do our part to help young people and the environment too!

Illustration Credits: Crafts prepared by June Ponte; craft photography by Carl Feryok; © 2004 JupiterImages, pp. 11 (photograph of girl), 21 (photograph of two boys), 23 (photograph of two boys), 31; Jupiterimages/Polka Dot/© Thinkstock, p. 17 (photograph of girl); wong sze yuen/iStock/© Thinkstock, p. 5.

Cover Illustration: Craft prepared by June Ponte; craft photography by Kristin McCarthy and Carl Feryok; Jupiterimages/Polka Dot/© Thinkstock (photograph of girl).

CONTENTS

Introduction 4

1. Bath Salts 6

2. Cupcake Magnets 8

3. Flower Photo Card 10

4. Decoupage Candy Cup 12

5. Handy Memo Book 14

6. Jewel Case Photo Frame 16

7. Garden in a Jar 18

8. Memory Plate 20

9. Jigsaw Puzzle Frame 22

10. Tulip Sun Catcher 24

Patterns 26
Read About Mother's Day 30
Index 32

Safety Note: Be sure to ask for help from an adult,
if needed, to complete these crafts!

INTRODUCTION

The second Sunday in May is a special day. It is Mother's Day! It is a day when we honor our mom. We give her cards, gifts, hugs, and kisses. We let her know how important she is to us.

The Mother's Day that we celebrate today began because of a woman named Anna Jarvis. She was very close to her mother. Anna Jarvis thought that all mothers should be honored with a special day.

Two years after her mother's death, Anna Jarvis decided to write letters to important people about her idea for a Mother's Day celebration. She wrote to ministers, businessmen, and lawmakers. Her friends helped her. In 1907, a special church service was held in memory of Anna Jarvis's mother. It was held in the church in Grafton, West Virginia, where her mother had attended.

Anna Jarvis wanted Mother's Day to become a national holiday. She kept writing letters about her idea. She wanted to have Mother's Day celebrated all across the United States. Finally, in 1914, President Woodrow Wilson made the holiday official.

He said that Mother's Day would be held every year on the second Sunday in May.

On Mother's Day, many people wear a red or white carnation flower. A red carnation is worn for a mother who is living. A white carnation is worn for a mother who has died. This custom began at the church service in Grafton for Anna Jarvis's mother. At the service, Anna Jarvis gave out white carnations. They were her mother's favorite flower.

Bath Salts

Your mom will love to relax in the bath with these soothing bath salts. Ask an adult to help you with this craft.

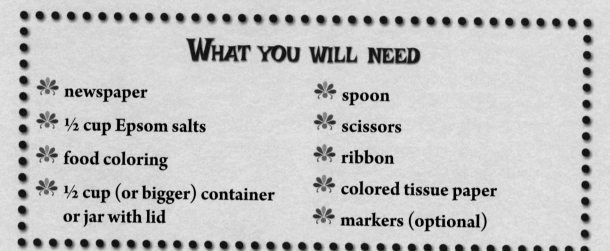

What You Will Need

- newspaper
- ½ cup Epsom salts
- food coloring
- ½ cup (or bigger) container or jar with lid

- spoon
- scissors
- ribbon
- colored tissue paper
- markers (optional)

What To Do

1. Cover your work space with newspaper.

2. Put Epsom salts and a drop of food coloring in a container or jar. Add a drop or two more if you want a darker color.

3. Mix them well with a spoon.

4. Put the lid on the container.

5. Wrap the container in tissue paper. Tie it with a ribbon. Trim the tissue wrapping if needed.

Make sure you have a clean jar . . .

Add the Epsom salts and coloring . . .

Decorate and finish with a bow!

HOLIDAY HINT:

Use a marker to write a Mother's Day message on the tissue paper wrapping. This will make your gift extra special.

Cupcake Magnets

Your mom will love these cupcake magnets. They do not have any calories or cause cavities!

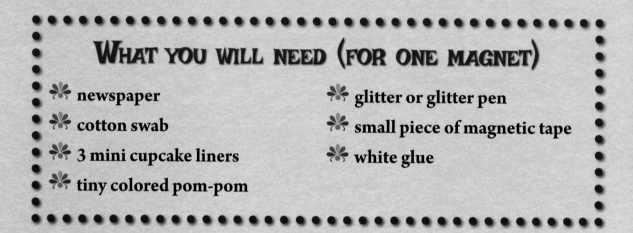

What you will need (for one magnet)

- newspaper
- cotton swab
- 3 mini cupcake liners
- tiny colored pom-pom
- glitter or glitter pen
- small piece of magnetic tape
- white glue

What to do

1. Cover your work space with newspaper.

2. Glue three mini cupcake liners together, one inside the other, to make one sturdy liner.

3. Glue the piece of magnetic tape to the bottom of the cupcake liner.

4. Glue the pom-pom in the center of the top liner.

5. Use the cotton swab to dot the pom-pom with glue.

6. Sprinkle on glitter. Let the glue dry. Shake off any loose glitter. If you wish, you may use a glitter pen instead.

Make sure you have everything . . .

Start by gluing the cupcake liners . . .

Glue the magnet on the bottom . . .

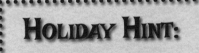

Your magnet is finished!

HOLIDAY HINT:

Make a few cupcake magnets. They make beautiful refrigerator magnets.

Flower Photo Card

You will be the center of the flower on this card. Mom will treasure this gift for years.

What You Will Need

- colored construction paper
- white glue
- 2 cupcake liners
- scissors
- green construction paper
- small photo of you (get permission first!)
- crayons and markers

What To Do

1. Fold the construction paper in half to form a card.

2. Flatten the cupcake liners. If you wish, cut one cupcake liner to look like a flower.

3. Glue one cupcake liner inside the other. Then glue the cupcake liners to the front of the card. This will be the flower.

4. Cut out a stem and leaves from the green construction paper. See page 26 for the pattern. Glue them on the card.

5. Glue your photograph in the center of the flower. Trim the picture if needed.

6. Decorate your card. Write messages to your mom on the inside and outside of the card.

Fold the paper
in half . . .

Cut out pieces for
the flower . . .

FOR MY MOM

HOLIDAY HINT:

Choose a photograph
of your brothers and
sisters, or your whole
family.

Decorate and give it
to your mom!

DECOUPAGE CANDY CUP

Decoupage is the art of gluing paper to a surface. Then the paper is sealed with something to give it a permanent finish.

WHAT YOU WILL NEED

- wax paper
- a yogurt or sour cream container or a small milk carton
- tissue paper
- white glue
- glue wash (2 tablespoons each of glue and water mixed together)
- paintbrush
- scissors
- candy
- colored plastic wrap (optional)
- pipe cleaner or ribbon (optional)

WHAT TO DO

1. Wash out your container well. Let it dry.

2. Cover your work space with wax paper.

3. Cut the tissue paper into small shapes.

4. Glue them on the container. Overlap the shapes to cover the container completely. Let them dry.

5. Brush the container with the glue wash. Let it dry.

6. Put some candy in the center of a piece of tissue paper or colored plastic wrap. Tie it with ribbon or a pipe cleaner.

7. Place the candy bundle in the container.

Start by cleaning the container . . .

Glue the tissue paper on the container . . .

Add the candy . . .

Your candy cup is complete!

HOLIDAY HINT:

When the candy is gone, your mom can use this decorated cup to hold pencils and pens.

Handy Memo Book

Mom will love this memo book for writing down addresses, recipes, or notes. She can add or remove pages whenever she wants.

What You Will Need

- 2 pieces of craft foam for the front and back covers
- white glue
- scissors
- small scraps of colored craft foam
- hole punch
- 10 index cards
- two ¾-inch binder rings

What to Do

1. Cut two pieces of craft foam 2 inches by 5 inches. This is the cover of your memo book.

2. Cut pieces of craft foam to make an interesting design for the front cover. You could make an animal, a flower, or even a word. For a flower, see page 27 for the pattern.

3. Glue the craft foam design on the front cover. Let the glue dry.

4. Punch holes in the top left and right corners of the front and back covers. You may need an adult to help line up the holes.

5. Cut index cards to fit inside the cover. Punch holes in each index card so that it matches up with the holes in both covers. Punch the holes one at a time. Ask an adult to help you if needed.

6. Loop a binder ring through each of the holes in the front cover, the index cards, and the back cover.

Start by cutting two
pieces of foam . . .

Cut out
the flower
pieces . . .

Cut the index
cards and
add holes . . .

Add rings and your
book is complete!

HOLIDAY HINT:

Write "I love you" on
the first page. Then
give the memo book
to your mom.

Jewel Case Photo Frame

Your mom can show off her family in this picture frame. It is small enough to take anywhere.

What You Will Need

- gift wrap paper
- CD jewel case
- 4-inch doily
- ribbon
- photograph of you or other family members (get permission first!)
- white glue

What To Do

1. Open the jewel case. Cut and trim two pieces of gift wrap paper to fit inside.

2. Glue the doily to one of the gift wrap pieces. Let it dry.

3. Glue the photograph in the center of the doily. Trim if needed. Let it dry.

4. Place the two pieces back to back inside the front cover of the jewel case. The piece with your photograph should be showing on the front.

5. Close the jewel case. Tie a ribbon around it and make a pretty bow.

Cut two pieces of gift wrap . . .

Add a doily . . .

Add a photograph
of yourself . . .

Slide it into the
jewel case . . .

HOLIDAY HINT:

Do you have a beloved family pet? Make a jewel case frame to display your animal's picture.

Your mom will love the frame!

Garden in a Jar

Mom will love this garden. She will never have to water it or weed it.

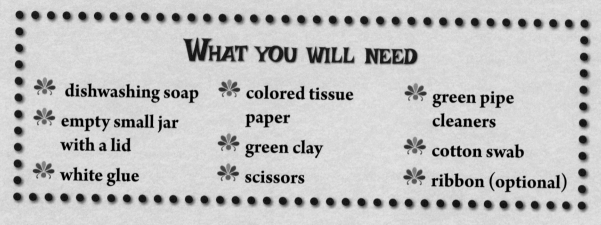

What you will need

- 🌸 dishwashing soap
- 🌸 empty small jar with a lid
- 🌸 white glue
- 🌸 colored tissue paper
- 🌸 green clay
- 🌸 scissors
- 🌸 green pipe cleaners
- 🌸 cotton swab
- 🌸 ribbon (optional)

What to do

1. Wash the empty jar and lid in warm soapy water. Remove the label. Let the lid and jar dry.

2. Place the lid topside down into the center of a small piece of tissue paper. Fold ends to cover the lid and glue. Let dry.

3. Put a ball of clay inside the center of the lid. Squish the ball down to leave a little space around the inside edges of the lid.

4. Cut tissue paper into long triangles about 4 inches by 1½ inches and roll up. See page 28 for the pattern. Twist one end tight. This will create the rosebuds.

5. Cut the pipe cleaners to fit in the jar for flowers stems. They can be cut different lengths.

6. Twist one end of the pipe cleaner around the twisted end of your rosebud. If you wish, use the cotton swab to glue the flower blossoms on the stems. Let them dry. Stick the stems in the clay.

7. Screw the lid on. Stand the jar on its lid so that the flowers are growing upward. If you wish, decorate the base with ribbon.

Start by washing an empty jar . . .

Cover the lid with tissue paper and fill with clay . . .

Cut pieces of tissue paper and make rosebuds . . .

Your flower garden will bloom all year!

HOLIDAY HINT:

Give the garden to your mom. This garden will bloom for her all year.

Memory Plate

Your mom can hang this gift someplace special. It will always remind her of you.

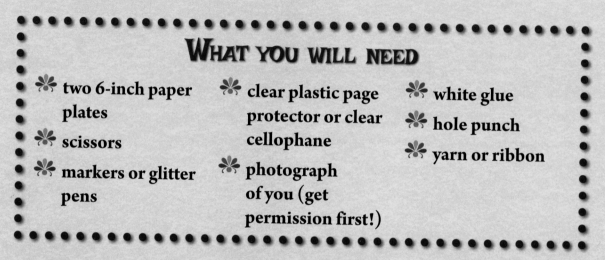

What you will need

- two 6-inch paper plates
- scissors
- markers or glitter pens
- clear plastic page protector or clear cellophane
- photograph of you (get permission first!)
- white glue
- hole punch
- yarn or ribbon

What to do

1. Cut out the center of one of the plates. Turn the plate over and decorate the edges. You will be decorating the edges on the back of the plate.

2. Cut a circular piece of clear plastic page protector or clear cellophane about ¼-inch bigger than the hole in the paper plate. Glue it to the inside of the paper plate. Let dry.

3. Cut construction paper to cover the center of the front of the second plate. Glue the construction paper to the center of the front of the plate.

4. Glue your photograph to the construction paper. If you wish, glue on ribbon roses or add other photos or mementos.

5. Punch a hole in the top of both plates. Place plates face to face. Line up the holes. Staple the plates together. Glue ribbon around the edge to cover the staples.

6. Thread the yarn or ribbon through the hole and tie.

Start by cutting the center out of a plate . . .

Add a photo and decorate . . .

Your memory plate is finished!

21

HOLIDAY HINT:

Choose photographs and mementos of special family times. Your mom will want to hang up this memory plate. It will bring back happy memories.

Jigsaw Puzzle Frame

Make a picture-perfect frame from craft sticks and puzzle pieces.

What you will need

- white glue
- four 6-inch craft sticks
- jigsaw puzzle pieces
- glue wash (2 tablespoons each of glue and water mixed together)
- paintbrush
- sheet of white paper
- photograph of you (get permission first!)
- scissors
- crayons or markers (optional)
- stickers or glitter (optional)

What to do

1. Glue the craft sticks together to form a frame. Let it dry.

2. Glue the puzzle pieces, blank side down, on the frame. Cover it completely. Let it dry.

3. Brush the glue wash over the puzzle pieces. Let them dry.

4. Cut the sheet of white paper to fit the back of the frame. On the front of the paper, glue your photograph in the center. Let it dry.

5. Glue the paper with your photograph to the back of the frame. Let it dry.

Glue your craft sticks together . . .

Add the paper backing . . .

Your mom will love the picture frame!

HOLIDAY HINT:

Turn the puzzle pieces over. Glue them to the frame, blank side up. You can write messages or decorate the blank side of the puzzle pieces to make a frame of your own design.

Tulip Sun Catcher

This sun catcher flower will decorate any window.

What You Will Need

- white glue
- 6-inch paper plate
- scissors
- tissue paper
- black construction paper
- hole punch
- ribbon

What To Do

1. Cut out the center of the paper plate. Set aside.

2. Place a design over black construction paper and trace, pressing down hard, around the design. See page 29 for the tulip pattern. On your black construction paper, cut out the shaded areas as shown on page 29. Or you can make your own design.

3. Cut out colored tissue paper and glue it to the back of the black construction paper.

4. Glue the tulip to a piece of tissue paper that is ¼-inch bigger than the hole in the paper plate. Let dry.

5. Glue the tissue paper, with the tulip glued to it, to the paper plate.

6. Punch a hole in the top of the plate. Thread ribbon through the hole and tie the ends in a bow. If you wish, punch holes around the plate and thread ribbon through the holes.

Cut a hole in
the plate . . .

Create a tulip
design . . .

Add colored tissue paper . . .

Your sun
catcher
looks
great!

HOLIDAY HINT:

Give the sun catcher
to your mom to hang
in a window. The sun
shining on the tulip
will brighten her day.

PATTERNS

Use tracing paper to copy the patterns on these pages. Ask an adult to help you cut and trace the shapes onto construction paper.

Make as large or
small as you want.

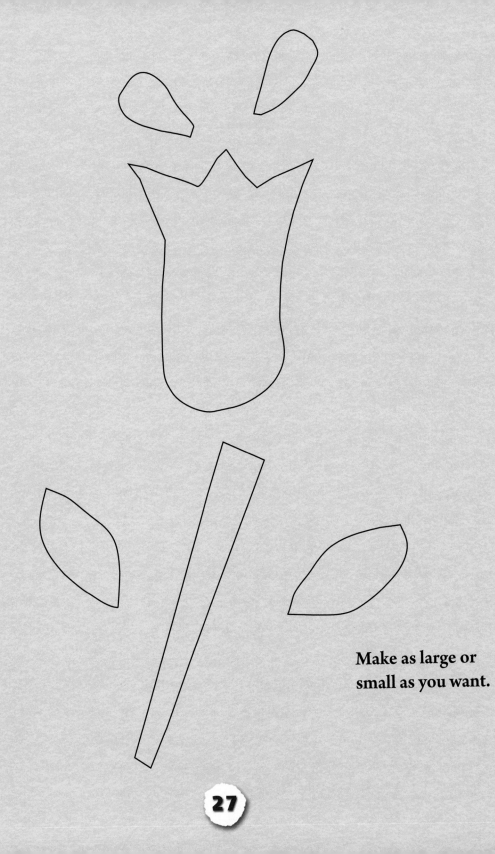

**Make as large or
small as you want.**

actual size

Cut out dark blue areas

Make as large or small as you want.

READ ABOUT MOTHER'S DAY

Gilpin, R. *Things to Make for Mother's Day*. London: Usborne, 2004.

Gore, Willma Willis. *Mother's Day*. Hillside, N.J.: Enslow Publishers, Inc., 1993.

Hughes, Monica. *Mother's Day*. Oxford: Heinemann Library, 2002.

Powell, Jillian. *Mother's Day*. London: Hodder Wayland, 2002.

INDEX

A
animal, 17

B
Bath Salts, 6–7
binder rings, 14

C
candy, 12, 13
carnations, 5
CD jewel case, 16
cellophane, 20
clay, 18, 19
construction paper, 10, 24
cotton swabs, 8, 18
craft foam, 14
craft sticks, 22, 23
crayons, 10, 22
cupcake liners, 8, 9, 10
Cupcake Magnets, 8–9

D
decoupage, 12
Decoupage Candy Cup,
    12–13
doily, 16, 17

E
Epsom salts, 6

F
Flower Photo Card, 10–11
food coloring, 6

G
Garden in a Jar, 18–19
gift wrap paper, 16, 17
glitter, 8, 22
glitter pens, 8, 20
glue, 8, 10, 12, 14, 16, 18,
    20, 22, 24
glue wash, 12, 22
Grafton, West Virginia, 4, 5

H
Handy Memo Book, 14–15
hole punch, 14, 20, 24

I
index cards, 14

J
jars, 6, 7, 18
Jarvis, Anna, 4, 5
Jewel Case Photo Frame,
    16–17
Jigsaw Puzzle Frame,
    22–23

M
magnetic tape, 8
markers, 6, 10, 20, 22
Memory Plate, 20–21
milk carton, 12

N
newspaper, 6

P
paintbrush, 12, 22
paper plates, 20, 24
patterns, 26–29
photographs, 10, 16, 20,
    22
pipe cleaners, 12, 18
plastic page protector, 20
plastic wrap, 12
pom-pom, 8

R
ribbon, 6, 12, 16, 18, 20, 24

S
scissors, 6, 10, 12, 14, 18,
    20, 22, 24
spoon, 6
stickers, 22

T
tissue paper, 6, 12, 13, 18,
    19, 24, 25
Tulip Sun Catcher, 24–25

W
wax paper, 12
white paper, 22
Wilson, Woodrow, 4

Y
yarn, 20